The Secret Sparkles Within

The Secret Sparkles Within

Demetri Welsh

DemetriWelsh.com

CONTENTS

In the heart of night, under the watchful gaze of a silvery moon, lies a world not far from your dream's balloon. A place where magic dusts the air, with auroras bright and rare—a land called Lumina, where every creature's fair. Here, within the Sparkle Grove's embrace, lies a secret, in a most enchanting space.

Listen close, for this tale's softly spun, of a journey under the stars and sun. A tale of discovery, bright and keen, through a world unseen, of a young girl named Lila, with eyes agleam. She felt quite ordinary, in every way, but in Lumina, she'd find her sparkle, come what may.

Guided by Ophelia, an owl wise and true, through a night where the world's painted anew. They'll meet creatures with sparkles that gleam and glow, teaching Lila more than she could ever know.

So turn the page, let your heart lead the way, and discover the sparkles that within you lay. For in Lumina's magic, so wild and free, you'll find the secret sparkles within thee.

Chapter 1: Lila's Wish

In a room, quiet, under the light of the moon,
Lila whispered to stars, a hopeful tune.

"Among all the wonders the world does keep,
I wish to find magic before I sleep."

Her room filled with glow, as if answering her plea,
And there, by her bed, stood an owl, wise as could be.

"I am Ophelia," said the owl with a bow,
"Come with me, Lila, there's something you should know."

2

Chapter 2: Journey to Lumina

With a flap and a flutter, they soared through the night,
To Lumina, a land where magic shone bright.

The sky danced with colors, vivid and wild,
Entrancing Lila, no longer just a child.

They landed softly in the Sparkle Grove, aglow,
Where creatures of magic freely did show.

"Each being here," Ophelia began to explain,
"Has a sparkle within, a unique domain."

Chapter 3: The Grove's Inhabitants

First, Freddie the firefly, with a flicker and flash,
Painted the night with a colorful splash.

Then Penelope parrot, with feathers so fine,
Whose melodies healed, note by note, line by line.

Each creature they met had a gift to share,
A sparkle unique, beyond compare.

Yet, Lila felt shadowed, a flicker in the dark,
Wondering quietly, "What is my spark?"

4

Chapter 4: The Mirror of Souls

Seeing her struggle, Ophelia led her to a glen,
Where the Mirror of Souls stood, revealing what's within.

"Not all sparkles are seen," the wise owl did say,
"Some shine from within, in their own special way."

Lila peered into the mirror, with a hesitant stare,
And saw not her reflection, but a light rare.

"It's your heart, your courage, your empathetic glow,
That's your sparkle, Lila, it's within you, you know."

Chapter 5: The Sparkle Unveiled

With newfound confidence, Lila returned to the grove,
Helping, understanding, letting her inner sparkle show.

She brought creatures together, with words kind and bright,
And in their unity, Lumina shone ever so light.

6

Chapter 6: Awakening

Lila awoke in her room, with the dawn's early light,
Her dream of Lumina still vivid and bright.

She carried her sparkle, no longer unseen,
Into her world, where she stood, brave and keen.

IN THE END ...

The Secret Sparkles Within

So, remember dear reader, as you close this book tight,
The sparkles within us all, shining so bright.

For like Lila, you too can discover your glow,
Your unique gift, that only you can show.

In the mystical land of Lumina, under the vast, starry sky,
The secret of sparkles within, forever will lie.

A reminder to all, both far and near,
The magic you seek is already here.